ORGANIZING A
LOCAL HISTORICAL SOCIETY

By Clement M. Silvestro

The American Association for State and Local History
Nashville, Tennessee

ORGANIZING A
LOCAL HISTORICAL SOCIETY

By Clement M. Silvestro[1]

Historical societies perform significant and valuable services to the community. Their primary concern is to preserve the historical record of the area in which they are located, and to keep alive the tradition and spirit of our national heritage. They rank among the oldest learned societies in the United States, and their research collections are major sources for the study of American history.

Historical societies attract members with varied backgrounds but their one common bond is their interest in local history. Their attributes—zeal, dedication, and perseverence—are responsible for the substantial contributions local historical society members have made to American historiography, historical preservation, and the development of our history museums. Who would venture to guess what number of historical documents, museum objects, or historic sites and buildings might have been forever lost if these men and women had not organized themselves into historical societies?

Traditionally, historical societies have collected and preserved the written records of the community—letters, diaries, journals, newspapers, and in some instances, local government documents. They have made these research materials available to writers, historians, genealogists, and to general readers who enjoy perusing books, faded documents, and yellowed newspapers for information about our past. From their research collections many societies have published important monographs, pioneer reminiscences, letters, diaries, and documents in book form or in a historical magazine, thus providing for the broad dissemination of their historical records.

Older historical societies, particularly those along the eastern seaboard and in the middle west, continue to maintain and

[1]The author is director of The Chicago Historical Society.

service research collections. But in the past few decades, with the strengthening of the major statewide and regional historical societies, with the development of national, state, and municipal archive programs, and with the growth of research centers in many college and university libraries, this important function, for obvious reasons, has been de-emphasized, and in some instances, even discontinued. However, many still maintain collections gathered by their predecessors, and continue to add to them. Moreover, historical society members frequently are the watchdogs in the community who locate important historical collections, and provide for their safety until they can be deposited in a statewide historical society or other appropriate repository.

If many local historical societies have limited their research library activities in recent years, they have made spectacular progress with other traditional functions: development of history museums; acceleration of informal education programs, including special projects for school children; and participation in the historic preservation movement. With assistance from organizations like the American Association for State and Local History and the American Association of Museums, local historical societies have refurbished their museums and made their exhibits more appealing. Their major collecting interest continues to be in the objects our forefathers made and used in their everyday living: furniture, clothing, woodenware, tinware, dishes and glassware, household utensils, farm equipment and simple machinery. Their popular exhibits have included the furnishings and stock of the old general store, a dentist's office, or that of a country doctor; an early newspaper and printing office; a rural schoolhouse, a blacksmith shop or early gristmill. All these re-creations vividly portray pioneer life in America, and help to visualize the environment in which our democratic institutions originated and developed.

Their iconographic collections—paintings, prints, and photographs—document events of the past and provide likenesses of prominent leaders. This rich illustrative material always captures attention at an exhibition, and it provides book and magazine publishers, newspaper and television writers, and authors excellent visual material for their projects.

History museums operated by local historical societies have become an important extension of America's educational system. Statewide historical societies and the American Association for State and Local History have laid the intensive groundwork of making teachers aware of the importance of utilizing the services of local historical societies in teaching local history. That teachers have come to recognize these benefits may be witnessed in the ever increasing numbers of school children who now visit local historical society museums, many of which offer guided tours, slide-lecture talks, and craft demonstrations for grade and high school students studying history. Some have made traveling exhibits available to the schools, and have distributed booklets and other publications on local history topics to supplement standard history textbooks, which seldom cover this subject adequately. No single development has been more significant to the local history movement than the projects for school groups.

In the field of historical preservation local historical societies have spearheaded projects that have won the respect and appreciation of their community. They have placed countless historical markers on sites and buildings recalling significant events and the people associated with these events. They have helped save from destruction numerous historic buildings, and helped to restore them either for functional use or as history museums. They have helped combat the bulldozers of city planners and urban renewal specialists who would have destroyed historic areas in towns and cities. They have been instrumental in formulating local and state legislation leveled to protect the historic character of their neighborhoods.

Informal education programs round out the activities of local historical societies—commemorating anniversaries of historic events, sponsoring lecture programs on local history and arranging for tours and pilgrimages to historic places. A variety of radio and television programs have been used effectively to bring local history to a larger audience. Development and refinement of these projects have made local historical societies important cultural and educational associations. The scope of their activities has assisted immeasurably toward nurturing a community spirit, fostering an allegiance to the values associated with our democratic way of life, and perpetuating the spirit that built America.

You who wish to form a historical society will derive useful knowledge and satisfaction from studying history at the local level. Many historians consider this the most logical approach and the best for a comprehensive understanding of the development of your own community. Who were the people who first settled the town, farmed the surrounding lands, sent their surpluses to distant markets, and floated bonds to bring in the railroads? Who were the men who mined the minerals, cut the timber, and built the mills that sawed the lumber? Who were the men who began small industries that developed into large manufacturing companies employing hundreds of workers? Who were the men and women who led the educational and religious life of the community, who built its schools and colleges? Who were the social and cultural leaders instrumental in developing libraries and art centers and in bringing music and the theater to your town? Who governed your town and represented its interests at the state capitol and in Congress? How do all these factors interact to make your community what it is today? How and why has your community changed through the years?

Exploring the byways of local history has become one of the most popular and absorbing forms of informal education in America. It has given adults who studied the generalizations of American history in textbooks the opportunity to learn about the actual situations from which these generalizations were drawn. For example, knowing the attitudes of the local Massachusetts merchants ard the English Navigation Acts and the practical problems colonials faced helps explain the causes of the American Revolution. Knowing the limitations of the tools and equipment of the pioneer farmer who pushed across the Appalachians to settle the Ohio and Kentucky valleys helps in understanding the hardships he had to endure and the courage he needed to face the dangers that awaited him. Knowledge of the importance of the cotton economy and the way of life of an antebellum town helps explain the firing on Fort Sumter. The letters and diaries of the Forty-niners preserved in a local historical society are rich in the details of the hardships of crossing the American continent. If you know the story of the development of individual industries in your own community, along with the growth of transportation, banking, and labor, you can better understand the industrial growth of the country as a whole.

You who are about to form a historical society will derive, besides knowledge and understanding, a great amount of enjoyment from your efforts. You need not be a trained historian to enjoy history any more than a trained horticulturist to grow fine roses or an expert philatelist to collect stamps. If you have interest, curiosity, enthusiasm, patience, and are willing to learn, you will find your efforts well worth the hard work necessary to form a successful historical society.

THE LOYAL ENTHUSIASTS

How *do* you go about establishing a local historical society? There are a variety of methods which have proved themselves for others. The organization of the Menasha (Wisconsin) Historical Society was largely the work of a single individual who fired the imaginations of a few close associates. Then, working together, they in turn stimulated a larger group to form their present organization. On the other hand, the organization of the El Paso (Texas) Historical Society was the work of the Women's Department of the Chamber of Commerce—1200 strong! With such a formidable and determined force, the ladies built up the membership of their local society to over 700 within a few short years.

More often, however, the impetus for establishing a local historical society is the work of a small group of five or six loyal enthusiasts, who are motivated to action by any number of events. The Vicksburg and Warren County (Mississippi) Historical Society was organized primarily to save the Old Court

House, a historic landmark in Vicksburg, from destruction. Interest in forming a county historical society in Winona, Minnesota, developed after a successful production of a historical pageant sponsored by a 4-H club. The exuberance and enthusiasm of centennial celebrations have prompted the formation of many a historical society, which has lasted far beyond the centennial event. Still others are formed to assume custodianship of historical materials turned over to a city or county by private citizens, or to care for the historical documents and materials of a defunct organization. Lastly, a historical society may be organized solely because a group of individuals wish to come together to study and appreciate the history of their community.

The immediate reason for forming a local historical society may be complex or simple, and the impetus for launching an organizing drive may stem from several sources. But whatever and whoever is responsibile for sparking the move, it will be the responsibility of a small group of people, planning and working together, to take the initiative in launching the drive. The local newspaperman, the high school teacher, the wife of the florist, the minister and his wife, and the electric appliance salesman may well constitute the key organizing group. All are intensely enthusiastic, and eager to be successful in their objective. To plot the establishment of a typical society, we shall assume we are addressing such a group of enthusiasts.

PRELIMINARY PLANNING

Americans are known to be organization prone. Thus organizing a local historical society should not present unusual difficulties, at least no more than those you might encounter if you were forming a rod and gun club or a fraternal organization. Certain basic procedures should be followed, however, and it will be the organizing group who will initiate them. In effect, the organizing group *is* the nucleus of the new historical society and it will be up to this group to develop an effective organization. Just how many preliminary meetings of the group will be necessary to lay the ground work for the formal organization of your society is directly proportional to the energy and drive of the organizing group. It may take one or two meetings, or five or six; but it is well to keep in mind that the more thorough the planning, the better the chances for ultimate success.

Select a temporary chairman and secretary the first time the organizing group meets. Frequently, the temporary chairman is the most promising candidate for the president of the society. He or she should have the necessary attributes for leadership, should be a person who can get things done, and especially important, one who can work with people. The temporary secretary should be chosen with the idea that the same person will fill the post after formal organization.

Before drawing up any elaborate plans, there are a few things your organizing group should consider. First, is there any existing organization in your area which performs functions similar to those you intend for your society? There may be an Old Settlers' Club or a Pioneer Association, founded many years ago. Upon investigation, you may find that it holds only one or two meetings a year and restricts membership to the descendants of the early settlers of your community. The restriction on membership imposed by Old Settlers' clubs has tended to be a factor in their decline, but there are still some in existence. A unique and highly successful one is the Society of California Pioneers at San Francisco. The Daughters of the Utah Pioneers and the Sons of the Utah Pioneers are two other successful groups. If an existing Old Settlers' Club should have an open membership, perhaps your group will want to unite with it and revitalize the association into a dynamic local historical society. But if the leadership in the organization is lethargic, and unresponsive to your constructive suggestions for enlarging and revitalizing their organization, undoubtedly it will be better to start your own society.

You may find that a local historical society already exists in your own county but that it has been inactive for many years. It will be wise to explore the circumstances responsible for its present dormant state and consider the possibilities for revitalizing it. Again, your group will have to weigh carefully the advantages and disadvantages involved in undertaking the job of instilling new life into a defunct organization. If the form of the organization is still intact, and if the obvious deficiency of the old society was inadequate leadership and drive, the merits of reorganizing the existing local society are considerable. It will take a great deal of tact and diplomacy to approach the members of a dying or defunct organization with proposals for reorganization. Chances are that once they have had an opportunity to evaluate your overtures, your suggestions will be readily received. But if your group decides that no existing historical agency will meet your needs, you are ready to form your own society.

When you have decided to proceed with your own organization, find out who can help you. Your state historical society, historical commission, or department of history and archives is the most convenient tap to the reservoir of mutual interests. Consult the latest edition of *Directory of Historical Societies and Agencies in the United States and Canada,* published by the American Association For State and Local History, Nashville, Tennessee, for the location and address of your statewide historical agency. Some state agencies have elaborate programs for assisting those who wish to form a local historical society, including field representatives who are experienced in working with local societies. They can be of invaluable assistance in planning a reasonable program in terms of resources and interests of the group. These same representatives can be of service in steering an embryonic society through incorporation, in drafting a constitution, and in laying the necessary foundations for future development.

Another important source of information on establishing a historical society is The American Association for State and Local History. The co-ordinating agency for local history in the United States and Canada, it serves its individual and institutional members as a professional leader and liaison. The Association stresses the proposition that the study of history on the local level is the best means for securing an understanding of our complex society and leads its members toward that end in their collecting, research, and publication. One of the sponsors of *American Heritage* magazine, it publishes *History News* (a monthly publication featuring current news and activities of state and local historical societies), and technical leaflets, dealing with many facets of historical society operation. Periodically, the Association publishes bulletins (such as this) written on subjects designed to guide and aid those working in state and local history. The Association's *Directory of Historical Societies and Agencies in the United States and Canada* periodically lists regional and local historical agencies in your area. New historical societies are welcome to join the Association, to enjoy the many benefits of membership, and to attend its annual meetings in different sections of the country.

Assistance may be available from still another source—state and regional federations of local historical societies. Oldest of these is the Pennsylvania Federation of Historical Societies, Harrisburg. There is the Bay State Historical League, Boston; more recently other leagues have been formed in states from California to Maine. Again, information about these leagues is found in the *Directory* of historical societies.

STATEMENT OF PURPOSE

Historical societies differ from all other special-interest groups in their specialized purposes. A clear concept and statement of purpose, therefore, is both a foundation of a local society and a guide for its future growth. Such a statement defines the scope of a society's activities and is the argument for recruiting members. It may be a very general statement, or it may specifically enumerate the projected activities. Although the immediate purpose for establishing your society may be very specific, such as to restore a historic house, or to operate a small museum in a room of the local library, in spelling out the purposes of your society it is better not to limit the scope of your activity to one particular function. If you are going to organize a local historical society, you should be ready to assume the responsibility for performing the functions of such a society. This is not to suggest that you must immediately do *all* of these things. It is merely a recognition that your group is aware of what a historical society does, and that as your organization grows and your program develops, you will want to undertake some of these other activities.

Still another reason for drafting an inclusive statement of purpose is to orient your society towards a well-rounded, balanced program. Such a society is more apt to be successful and can more easily satisfy the desires of a larger membership of diverse interests. In addition, if the time should come when you are seeking financial support either from individuals or the community, it will be to your advantage to have a broad, inclusive program which will win community support. Therefore, whether or not your group intends to engage in a wide range of historical society functions immediately, it is best to include all the important activities of the strong historical society in the statement of purpose.

There is no need to employ fancy or elaborate prose to explain the reason for your existence. Be simple and to the point. Following is a sample statement of purpose for your society:

The purpose of the Lakeville County Historical Society is to bring together those people interested in history, especially in the history of our community. Understanding the history of our community is basic to our democratic way of life, gives us a better understanding of our state and nation, and helps us better to appreciate our American heritage.

The society's major function will be to discover and collect any material which may help to establish or illustrate the history of the county: its exploration, settlement, development, and activities in peace and in war; its progress in population, wealth, education, arts, science, agriculture, manufactures, trade, and transportation. It will collect printed material such as histories, genealogies, biographies, descriptions, gazetteers, directories, newspapers, pamphlets, catalogues, circulars, handbills, programs, and posters; manuscript material such as letters, diaries, journals, memoranda, reminiscences, rosters, service records, account books, charts, surveys, and field books; and museum material such as pictures, photographs, paintings, portraits, scenes, aboriginal relics, and material objects illustrative of life, conditions, events, and activities of the past or the present.

The society will provide for the preservation of such material and for its accessibility, as far as may be feasible, to all who wish to examine or study it; co-operate with officials in insuring the preservation and accessibility of the records and archives of the county and of its cities, towns, villages, and institutions; and insure the preservation of historic buildings, monuments, and markers.

The society will disseminate historical information and arouse interest in the past by publishing historical material in the newspapers or otherwise; by holding meetings with pageants, addresses, lectures, papers, and discussion; by marking historic buildings, sites, and trails; and by using the media of radio and television to awaken public interest.

The society will co-operate with the state historical society [state historical commission, or state department of archives and history] to collect and preserve materials of state-wide significance so that these materials can be made available to students and scholars.

If funds are available, by all means have your statement of purpose printed, either in the original form or in a revision adapted to meet special needs. It can be distributed to the press and radio as a news announcement or as a special feature story on the movement to form a local historical society. It can be mailed directly to likely membership prospects during the organizational drive. If printing costs are out of your reach, investigate other less expensive duplicating processes such as mimeographing. Listing in a written form the salient reasons for organizing a society will be a useful ready reference to the organizing group when it goes out to persuade others to join.

REGIONAL LIMITS

A question you should consider at the pre-organization meeting relates to the regional limits of your society. There may be factors attending the organization of your society that will predetermine the question for you. If you happen to be revitalizing a dormant historical society, which already has definite geographic limits specified in its charter, the question may never come up. But for any number of reasons, you may be faced with the decision of whether your historical society should be municipal, township, or county. All three types exist throughout the United States, for there seems to be a natural relationship between the unit of government and the geographic limits of a historical society. But regional limits do not necessarily determine the size of the organization; there are some municipal historical societies that have larger physical plants, budgets, staffs, programs, and even holdings than some state historical societies. The Dallas, Buffalo, and Detroit historical societies are among the larger municipal organizations.

Societies serving a smaller municipal area, such as a town or township, are common in New England, where the township system of government predominates. In some instances two, three, or even four towns have joined together to form a society. Towns with an unusually rich historic heritage, such as Plymouth, Massachusetts, and Charleston, South Carolina, confine the geographic limits of their societies to the immediate region.

Outside New England and especially in the West and South, the county is the more common unit of local government and of organization for a historical society. A perusal of local historical societies in the American Association's *Directory* indicates the county historical society is the most popular form. This is the case even in areas where political boundaries, arbitrarily drawn, frequently violate geographic factors responsible for making neighboring communities economically and socially interdependent.

In dealing with the problem of historical society representation, make every effort to draw members from throughout the county. Many county societies succumb to the practice of making the county seat or principal city the sole center of activity, and residents of that immediate area have a tendency to dominate the membership rolls and the society program. The hinterland is also important in local history, and if residents of *all* towns and cities in a county participate in the local society, richer and more worthwhile historical contributions can be made.

TIMING

Another important factor you must consider in making plans for organization is timing. When is the best time to organize a local historical society? Obviously, there is no set rule, but certainly you would avoid trying to launch a new organization during the December holiday season, or during the summer months when many people are on vacation. Any other time during the year should be perfectly acceptable, depending always upon local conditions. However, community mood is an important factor to consider when organizing a local historical society. Centennial celebrations present an ideal community mood in which to launch an organization. Centennial promotions alert the whole community to its history; young men grow beards; and stovepipe hats and period dresses are hauled out of attic trunks. Stores display prints, pictures, and etchings of Main Street as it appeared 100, 200, or 300 years ago. The press and radio constantly refer to the event and the newspapers publish centennial editions. A historical society not only fits admirably into the centennial production, but the embryonic society can directly benefit from the historical interest created by the centennial. Fairs, anniversaries of historical events, and institutional centennials are other occasions that may be utilized to launch a historical society.

Unexpected factors might determine the time for organizing your society. The hasty condemnation of a historic section of your community by city or county officials to make way for a new housing development or a new highway may provoke a sufficient number of indignant citizens to start a historical society in order to prevent such hasty condemnation proceedings in the future. Occasionally, the razing of old sections of your town or city to make way for new buildings uncovers a significant number of historical artifacts, arouses an interest in the community's history, and stimulates a group of people to form a historical society. Whatever the case, timing depends upon local conditions. Use good judgment and imagination in selecting the time to launch your organizational drive.

PLANNING THE ORGANIZATIONAL MEETING

After your group has decided on the time to launch an organizational meeting, has drawn up a statement of purpose, and has defined the regional limits of the society, you may begin to make arrangements for the organizational meeting. Planning is most important. Set the date and hour, and arrange for a place to meet. Until now your group has probably met in the home of one of the members; a public building is better than a private home for the organizational meeting and all future meetings. If your group has no money, you must use ingenuity in acquiring a place which is available free of charge. The advantage is with you; for your cause is a worthy one and your request is likely to be received sympathetically. The local library is an excellent place if it has a meeting room. The county court house or a local school are possibilities also. A local church will certainly allow you to meet at its quarters for one or two meetings. Finding a permanent home for your association will be a primary order of business after you are organized, and with a proper presentation to the responsible officials of the purpose and functions of your local historical society, it is very likely that you can secure a room in some public building.

PROGRAMMING THE ORGANIZATIONAL MEETING

What type of a program should you have for your organizational meeting? You must keep in mind that the purpose of this first meeting is to convince those people interested in history to join you in forming a local historical society. You will want to have the kind of program that will make those attending eager to become members of your organization. A good organizational meeting should open with a brief, convincing talk by the temporary chairman, explaining why you want to organize a local historical society. Essentially, he should incorporate the ideas you have already drawn up in the statement of purpose, with a few concrete examples to illustrate the significant points. He should not speak longer than ten or fifteen minutes.

The second part of the program should be aimed at kindling the flames of enthusiasm to the point of action. You might call upon the services of your state historical society to help you with this part of the program. Perhaps you can arrange to have the director of the state historical society speak. If he is not available, he may be able to send you someone connected with his organization who can stimulate your people to action. Some state historical agencies have excellent movies or slide-lecture talks designed to be shown at just such organizational meetings.

If you are in a college or university community you may secure aid from a faculty member of the history department. Most historians appreciate the importance of local history and will be happy to accommodate and co-operate with your group.

Whatever program you schedule for the organizational meeting, place the emphasis on quality rather than quantity. For after presenting the argument and the possibilities for the society, there remains the business aspect of forming the society, and if not well executed, the flame of optimistic enthusiasm may be extinguished by the cold wind of reality.

PUBLICITY FOR THE ORGANIZATIONAL MEETING

The program has been prepared; the time, place and date of the organizational meeting have been arranged. Now, there is the problem of publicizing the fact that you are forming a society and, equally important, notifying likely prospects for membership. If, as is frequently the case, one of your organizing group is on the staff of one of the local newspapers, your publicity problems are solved. Newspaper men frequently have a good grounding and a keen interest in history. If you are not so fortunate as to have a newsman in your group, arrange to notify the press, radio, and television with information about your first meeting. It is a newsworthy event and it will be given attention.

Publicity for the organizational meeting through the press and radio should be supplemented by direct personal contact with individuals. First, obtain the support of public officials and leading citizens of your town, county, or city in order to secure for your project public approval. Write to the civic leaders explaining your project and asking them for their support, preferably by written testimonials. Then, make direct contacts with service organizations such as the Rotary, Lions, Kiwanis, and Women's clubs, and veterans and civic organizations. In addition to receiving official support from such groups, you will find some of their members eager to join your society. Since local historical societies are educational agencies, you should strive to win the support of the school and library officials of town and county. Again, the contacts you make here may win you active members among teachers and librarians interested in history.

Now you are ready to solicit directly the people you think might wish to become active members. When approaching people for membership it is important to realize that interest in local history transcends all occupational, nationality, or religious boundaries. Membership in local societies should encompass as many different groups as possible—doctors, lawyers, teachers, laborers, housewives, farmers, clergymen, and businessmen. All of these and other occupational groups can be found in the ranks of the successful local historical society. To reach all of these groups, make personal contacts, call people on the phone, and present your proposal to the widest possible audience. Persuade them all to come to your organizational meeting.

Most of the members of the immediate organizing group will know one or two people who should be interested in becoming members. This is not enough. Who are likely prospects for membership? Almost anyone and everyone! While scouting around, you are likely to discover some rewarding situations. It may disarm you to learn that for years the janitor at one of the county schools has been collecting artifacts of the early settlers in your region, from farming tools to household supplies. His collection has grown so large that he seeks special arrangements to house it. The retired doctor in your town, who is credited with delivering about half of the population, has been doing research on the history of your community since long before he quit his practice. He is now ready to write a book. The owner of the local hardware store is an enthusiastic and serious student of Indians. He not only has made an independent study of the major tribes that inhabited your area, but he has also collected many Indian artifacts. Mrs. Longly and Mrs. Wentworth, both housewives with grown children, would be eager and active members of your group. Both majored in history in college, but until now growing families prevented their indulging their interest. The principal of the local high school, you learn, is an enthusiastic student of Civil War history. His great-grandfather fought at Gettysburg, and he owns a collection of letters describing army life in the war. The principal also has the letters his great-grandmother wrote to her soldier husband, which give a good account of how the war affected life in your small community. He is a good candidate for your society. Convince the people you approach that they do not have to be professional historians to be local society members. All of the members will study and learn together.

Do not make the mistake of thinking that a member of a local historical society is not worth his salt unless he himself is an "old-timer"; make an effort to invite people of all ages. To be sure, many older men and women do have a perspective born of experience, which, in turn, tends to make them more aware of the importance of history. But increasingly, younger people are developing avaricious appetites for history. They are as eager to learn how and why their region developed as are the old-timers. The broader the social, economic, and occupational base of membership, the more stable your historical society is apt to be.

THE ORGANIZATIONAL MEETING

The first formal meeting can make or break the aspirations of those who are forming a historical society. Carry out your program with zest and enthusiasm. Your organizing group has spent many hours preparing for the meeting, and this is the night when the careful planning should pay off. It might be advantageous to have for this initial meeting a temporary display of old photographs of the community and of early settlers. Before starting, have your guests try to identify the places and people in them. A few unusual museum objects might also serve as conversation pieces. It is also an excellent way to get people acquainted and interested. As previously arranged, the temporary chairman opens the meeting with a few brief remarks stating the reasons why your community should have a historical society and what kind of activities it should intend to support. The remarks can be an informal presentation of the statement of purposes previously drafted. Move along with dispatch and introduce your main speaker, who should have been previously asked to limit his talk to thirty minutes.

At the conclusion of the address, and after thanking the speaker, the chairman announces that he will entertain a motion to organize the local historical society. A member of the organizing group rises and is recognized by the chairman. He may either informally present a motion to the effect, or he can read a short prepared statement taken from the statement of purpose and embodying the motion to organize. After another member of the organizing group seconds the motion, the chairman then throws open the motion to discussion. If there are lovable but long-winded enthusiasts present, the chairman must tactfully but firmly keep the floor open for others to be heard. He should encourage the widest possible expression of views of the prospective members, for an artificially imposed society will not long endure. A few words from the leading citizens of the community would likewise aid the cause. The temporary chairman should solicit letters from prominent civic leaders and service organizations endorsing your proposal to form a society, and read these at the meeting. After suitable discussion, put the motion to a vote. You can probably assume that no one at the meeting will be opposed to organizing a local historical society; otherwise, he would not have come in the first place. The only possible opposition to your project is likely to come from a nearby historical society that feels another such group threatens its activity. You should have the answers ready if there is a possibility of such opposition.

After the motion to organize is passed, you are ready to forge ahead. You are far from achieving an established historical society, but the machinery is well in motion. You should not expect to accomplish too much at the organizational meeting, and it is best not to try. A member of the organizing group should propose a motion empowering the temporary chairman to appoint a Committee on Organization, responsible for drafting a constitution and the bylaws, to be presented at the next meeting. In appointing people to the committee, the temporary chairman should make sure that it includes some members attending for the first time. It is important to draw these new people into the organizing program of the local historical society immediately so that they will feel welcome as a part of the new organization. It is also important to appoint to the Committee on Organization persons who are familiar with the procedures for drawing up rules and regulations for clubs or societies. A lawyer, teacher, writer, or librarian may be very helpful in this activity.

Before you adjourn the first meeting be sure to set the time, place, and date for the second meeting, about three weeks hence. Also, have the temporary secretary obtain the names, addresses, and phone numbers of all those who attended and expressed an interest in joining your society. After these details are completed, call for a motion to adjourn, and spend the remainder of the evening chatting with the people present. Introduce the potential members individually to the guest speaker. If you do serve refreshments, keep them simple. Reserve dinners, pot-luck suppers, and outdoor picnics for later special occasions after the group is better organized and acquainted.

COMMITTEE WORK

After your organizational meeting, the important work shifts from the original group to the Committee on Organization. The committee must draw up the rules and regulations under which the society will operate, usually in the form of articles of incorporation or a constitution. The procedural details for operating the society are incorporated in a set of bylaws. The fundamental rules of your society should be inclusive enough to meet the needs ·of the organization but should avoid complexities and rigidities, which tend to confuse. The Committee on Organization may decide to draw up a constitution or it may decide in favor of incorporation. While large organizations may wish to do both, one or the other is sufficient for a local historical society. And, though it is more complex, organizing under articles of incorporation has many tangible advantages.

INCORPORATION AND ITS BENEFITS

Why is it better to incorporate? You will save yourself innumerable legal headaches if you do. Most important of many advantages is that under the law, the local society becomes a legal person; members of the society will be immune from individual liability, be it from society debts, or other unforeseeable legal action against your group. Another advantage is that by incorporating, the society will enjoy perpetual existence. All historical societies plan to collect historical materials, such as manuscripts or museum objects. Under articles of incorporation, title to such property is held in the name of the society, and it will be protected against falling into the hands of individual members in the event the society should ever dissolve.

Incorporation gives your society legal status, and it is only on such basis that many potential donors will make gifts to your organization. You can never know just when a benefactor may decide to give your society a valuable collection of materials or property for a local museum. It is best to be prepared to receive such bequests.

Lastly, incorporation is, in effect, state recognition of your society; there is a certain amount of prestige in having your organization incorporated.

How do you go about incorporating your local historical society? Most states have special statutes that govern the formation of non-profit organizations. These laws vary from state to state, and are changed from time to time. Check at your local library for the procedure in your state for incorporating an organization. There you will find reference volumes on the subject of organizing clubs which discuss the subject thoroughly. Write to the office of the secretary of state at your state capitol for additional information and the necessary forms for application. If the legal jargon baffles you, you might engage a competent lawyer and arrange for him to draw up the incorporation papers. Since it is a legal document, it must be technically correct and in proper form. But even before taking this action, you may want to check with your state historical society for advice. Some state societies arrange the details of incorporation for local societies that plan to affiliate with the state organization. (See Appendix I for a sample set of incorporation papers.)

AFFILIATION

There are two questions akin to that of incorporation: affiliation with the state society, and taxation. Affiliation with a state historical society is not standard procedure throughout the United States, but in those states where such a direct relationship does exist, it has proved mutually beneficial. Oregon, Minnesota, and Wisconsin are among the states that have successful programs of affiliation, and these arrangements are generally included in the articles of incorporation as a special section. Your state historical society will be happy to consult regarding affiliation clauses.

The main purpose of affiliation is to establish a mutual exchange of information and reciprocal assistance between the local society and the state society. It does not imply that the state organization in any way interferes with, or dominates, the activities of the local society. The only requirement of an affiliated society under most arrangements is that it submit a brief annual report of its activities to the state society. Also under the arrangement, in some cases, the state society assumes ownership of the collections of the local historical society should the organization dissolve, and acts as guardian of the collections should there be any temporary disruption of the organization. Affiliation is thus a safeguard for valuable historical records and materials. In return, the local society may solicit advice and information from the state society on any of the many problems that inevitably arise. Affiliation with a state historical agency is a convivial arrangement for two organizations engaged in activities with the same purpose and obligation.

TAXATION

Local historical societies incorporated as not-for-profit educational institutions may be declared tax exempt organizations under Section 501 (c) (3) of the United States Internal Revenue Code of 1954. The fact that your society is organized as a not-for-profit corporation under the laws of your state does not automatically entitle it to this privilege. Formal application must be filed with the Internal Revenue Bureau. The society cannot claim this status until the Internal Revenue Bureau grants the privilege in a formal letter. The four requirements for exemption are: (a) It must be organized and operated exclusively for one or more of the enumerated purposes; (b) No part of its earnings may inure to the benefit of any private shareholder or individual; (c) No substantial part of its activities may include propaganda, or otherwise attempt to influence legislation; (d) It may not participate or intervene in any political campaign on behalf of any candidate for public office.

Exempt status is vital to a thriving historical society and for this reason the organizing committee should be aware of its importance. Foremost is the fiscal noninterference by the U. S. government, the most important concept of which is that the Internal Revenue Bureau cannot tax the income of your society. The second important characteristic is that tax exempt status will permit donors to deduct from their federal income tax (to the limit allowable under the law) gifts of money, real estate, bonds, stocks, and other chattel property they may wish to give your society. It also permits them to deduct from their federal income tax the fair market value (determined by a qualified, independent appraiser) of library, museum and art objects they may give to your society.

As soon as all signs indicate that you have a going organization it would be wise to make a formal application for tax exempt status. It may be prudent to engage the services of an attorney to expedite your application although it is entirely possible to file one without his services. To apply for tax exempt status, the principal officer of the historical society should obtain from the U. S. Internal Revenue Bureau Form 1024, the standard application form used by religious, charitable, scientific, literary, and educational organizations. After it is properly filled out, return the form to the Internal Revenue Bureau. In recent years the U. S. government has reviewed these applications with greater scrutiny so do not be alarmed if a few months pass before you receive your exemption letter. In most instances, once the ruling is received, the exemption is effective from the date of formation of the organization.

To maintain and safeguard your tax exempt status the society must file annually with the U. S. Internal Revenue Bureau a financial report on Form 990A. This form, available from the U. S. Internal Revenue Bureau, is due on or before the fifteenth day of the fifth calendar month following the close of your society's taxable year. Tax exempt status is a valuable asset. Do not jeopardize it by failing to comply with the legal requirements.

CONSTITUTION

The Committee on Organization may decide to postpone incorporation until the society is well on its feet and has a well-rounded program in operation. If this should be the case, the committee will draw up a constitution as the basis for organization. The constitution is the fundamental law of your society; it should not be cluttered with detailed rules. (See Appendix II for a sample form of a constitution.)

If your society decides to have an affiliation agreement with your state historical society, commission, or department of archives and history, this agreement should be included as an article in your constitution. You will have to arrange with your state historical agency the terms of the affiliation, and draw up an article for the constitution embodying the terms of the agreement. The state historical agencies that do have affiliation agreements with local historical societies usually have a standard agreement, but it does vary.

In addition, your local society may wish to have another article in the constitution governing the disposition of the collections should the group ever dissolve. If you have an affiliation agreement with your state historical agency, most likely it will cover the disposition of the collections. If not, your local society may draw up an article designating a successor to receive its collections. The collections should go to the local library, a school, the historical society in a neighboring county or municipality, or to a state historical agency, where they may be properly cared for.

BYLAWS

The bylaws specify the details of organization and procedure, and every organization needs them to govern its deliberations. There should be nothing in the bylaws contradicting the articles of incorporation or the constitution, whichever document your group has for its organic law, and bylaws should be flexible enough to facilitate an efficient operating procedure. (See Appendix III for a sample set of bylaws.) The Committee on Organization should have the constitution and bylaws ready to submit to the society's second organizational meeting. If it is possible it will be helpful to have them duplicated and mailed to the members before the meeting so that they may have a chance to read and study them beforehand.

CLASSES OF MEMBERSHIP AND DUES

Under the bylaws, classes of membership and dues should be carefully defined. Dues may be varied to suit local conditions, and the amount of dues paid by a member should not determine that person's degree of activity and relative voice in the society and its undertakings. A schedule of dues is not a system of discrimination, but merely a device to tailor the dues to pocketbooks in order that all who want to participate in historical society activity may do so, regardless of economic standing in the community.

The simplest of all arrangements is to have one class of membership and one rate for everyone. More and more, however, local historical societies throughout the country are finding that it is advantageous to have several categories of membership. A historical society is an educational institution which solicits civic groups, service or fraternal organizations, and business firms to make financial contributions for the benefit of the society. For these groups the historical society should have a business and professional membership, usually at $15.00 per year, and a sustaining membership category at $50.00 or $100.00 per year.

A society may also have several classes of membership for individuals. An annual membership can be set anywhere from

$1.00 to $5.00. For persons who can afford to make more substantial financial contributions to the society, contributing and life memberships should be available. Contributing memberships should start at a figure above the annual memberships. Thus, if annual membership is only $1.00, contributing membership can start at $5.00; if annual membership starts at $5.00, contributing membership can start at $10.00 or $25.00. A life membership must be paid in one lump sum, and is restricted to individual persons, never being sold to institutions or business firms. The dues for a life membership are usually $100.00, for the funds are usually invested, and the annual interest should equal the annual membership fee.

COMMITTEES

In drawing up the bylaws, the Committee on Organization has the choice of empowering the president and/or board of directors to appoint as many standing committees as may be deemed advisable for administering society functions and activities. Or, as an alternative, the Committee on Organization may wish to incorporate into the bylaws a specific number of standing committees. These standing committees may be established at the time of organization whether or not the society is actually ready to take on a broad program. For example, your society may not be contemplating any publication program for the time being, but it is advisable to establish a standing committee to direct this important society function. Its immediate purpose may be to determine when the society should undertake publication and to find the way to produce and finance the published works. If the Committee on Organization chooses to include them in the bylaws, the following standing committees are suggested:

A. Library Committee—responsible for the collection, cataloging, care, arrangement, and repair of books, manuscripts, newspapers, and other library materials.

B. Museum Committee—responsible for the collection, cataloging, cleaning, repair, care, and storage of historic objects; for arranging museum exhibits and for the correct historic interpretation of these exhibits; for the care and upkeep of museum quarters.

C. Publications Committee—responsible for finding ways and means for publishing information and research studies in a newsletter to members, in a quarterly bulletin, and as books; for publicity; for producing radio and television programs.

D. Historic Sites Committee—responsible for establishing the historic validity of sites proposed for marking; for marking historic sites; for arranging historical tours.

E. Program Committee—responsible for arranging suitable programs; for setting time, place, and date of meetings.

F. Membership Committee—responsible for membership drives and for processing applications for membership.

G. Nominations Committee—responsible for making nominations for officers and members of the board of directors.

There is generally no pressing need for a Finance Committee; the treasurer usually can handle routine money matters of a small organization. However, if your organization owns real estate or chattel property, or if your society is planning an extensive fund-raising drive for purchasing a historic house or quarters for a museum, you may wish to establish a separate Finance Committee.

SECOND MEETING

The second meeting of your local historical society should be devoted to the problems of formal organization. Remember that this meeting is as important as the first, and good planning is again essential. The temporary chairman of the society should have made arrangements for a place to meet, preferably the same as the first meeting. The temporary secretary will have sent out notices of the meeting by mail to those who attended the first meeting. In addition, the temporary chairman, assisted by other members of the original organizing group, will cooperate to promote interest in the meeting. They should send notices of the meeting to the local newspapers and to the radio stations. A visit to the newspaper editor might result in a sympathetic editorial in the local paper encouraging the new society. Phone persons who did not attend the first meeting but who might be interested in joining. Publicity is always important, for it is the best means of attracting new members.

The temporary chairman opens the meeting, and requests the temporary secretary to read the minutes of the previous meeting. After the minutes have been approved, the chairman calls for a report from the Committee on Organization. The chairman of the committee reads the articles of incorporation, or constitution, whichever fundamental document has been chosen, and moves its adoption. After the motion has been seconded, the proposition is open for discussion. If copies of the proposed document have been distributed to the members, the work of amending and ratifying will be much more simple. After the adoption of the basic document, the same procedure should be followed for the bylaws.

You may be able to dispense with the two major items of business in a short time, or they may take you a good portion of the evening. If you have a verbose, strong-minded group, allow enough time for all to air their views. It requires patience to listen, but in the long run you will have a happier family. Once the organic law of the historical society has been adopted and the bylaws have been accepted, your society is ready to operate under the procedure prescribed in these documents.

The membership, acting as a committee of the whole, can appoint a nominating committee to present a slate of officers and candidates for the board of directors for the next meeting. The highlight of the next meeting of the new local historical society, after the election, will likely be the installation of the officers with appropriate ceremonies at which both officers and members reaffirm their pledge to carry out the aims and objectives of the new local historical society.

The procedure for organizing a local historical society described here is designed to be used only as a guide. Organization will not always follow a clear-cut pattern. It may be possible to accomplish the necessary steps in two or three meetings, or it may take longer. Whatever the case, organizational procedures can and should be kept flexible and informal. The form of organization is meant to be a piece of serviceable machinery to make it easier for your group to function and to carry on your activities. Do not become slaves to the form of organization or to parliamentary procedure; it may have a stifling effect upon your organization. A good plan of organization will help you to have a good society, but organization in itself will not make the society. The members themselves will determine that. They must have enthusiasm, determination, willingness to work, and affection for the kind of work they are doing. These are the ingredients which make a successful society.

Perhaps your local library will have supplementary materials dealing with the problems of organizing a society. Your state historical agency may be able to offer you some assistance. If you need further help please write to The American Association for State and Local History. It will be happy to attempt to answer your questions.

Good luck!

APPENDIX I

SAMPLE ARTICLES OF INCORPORATION

ARTICLE I

The name of the corporation shall be [official name of the organization].

ARTICLE II

The period of existence shall be perpetual.

ARTICLE III

The business and purpose of this corporation shall be to bring together those people interested in history, and especially in the history of [specified region]. Understanding the history of our community is basic to our democratic way of life, gives us a better understanding of our state and nation, and promotes a better appreciation of our American heritage.

The corporation's major function will be to discover and collect any material which may help to establish or illustrate the history of the area: its exploration, settlement, development, and activities in peace and in war; its progress in population, wealth, education, arts, science, agriculture, manufactures, trade, and transportation. It will collect printed material, such as histories, genealogies, biographies, descriptions, gazetteers, directories, newspapers, pamphlets, catalogs, circulars, handbills, programs, and posters; manuscript material such as letters, diaries, journals, memoranda, reminiscences, rosters, service records, account books, charts, surveys, and field books; and museum material such as pictures, photographs, paintings, portraits, scenes, aboriginal relics, and material objects illustrative of life, conditions, events, and activities of the past and the present.

The society will provide for the preservation of such material and for its accessibility, as far as may be feasible, to all who wish to examine or study it, to co-operate with officials in insuring the preservation and accessibility of the records and archives of the county and of its cities, towns, villages, and institutions, and to undertake the preservation of historic buildings, monuments, and markers.

The society will disseminate historical information and arouse interest in the past by publishing historical material in the newspapers or otherwise; by holding meetings with pageants, addresses, lectures, papers, and discussion; by marking historic buildings, sites, and trails; and by using the media of radio and television to awaken public interest.

ARTICLE IV

The location of the principal office shall be [city and state].

ARTICLE V

The name of the initial registered agent is [an official of the society].

ARTICLE VI

The address of the initial registered agent is [address of the society's registry official].

ARTICLE VII

The board of directors shall have the power to conduct all affairs of the society. The number of the board of directors shall be fixed by bylaw but shall not be less than three. The manner of election or appointment and the term of office of members of the board of directors shall be that stated in the bylaws.

ARTICLE VIII

The society shall have one or more classes of membership. The designation of such classes, and the qualifications, rights, and method of acceptances of members of each class, shall be specified in the bylaws.

ARTICLE IX

This corporation shall not have or issue shares of stock and it shall pay no dividends or pecuniary profits whatever to its organizers or members, although it may confer benefits upon members in conformity with its purposes and the law.

ARTICLE X

These articles may be amended in the manner authorized by law at the time of amendment.

APPENDIX II

SAMPLE CONSTITUTION

ARTICLE I
Name

The name of this society shall be [official name of the organization].

ARTICLE II
Purpose

The purpose of this society shall be to bring together those people interested in history, and especially in the history of [specified region]. Understanding the history of our community is basic to our democratic way of life, gives us a better understanding of our state and nation, and promotes a better appreciation of our American heritage.

The society's major function will be to discover and collect any material which may help to establish or illustrate the history of the area: its exploration, settlement, development, and activities in peace and in war; its progress in population, wealth, education, arts, science, agriculture, manufactures, trade, and transporation. It will collect printed material such as histories, genealogies, biographies, descriptions, gazetteers, directories, newspapers, pamphlets, catalogs, circulars, handbills, programs, and posters; manuscript material such as letters, diaries, journals, memoranda, reminiscences, rosters, service records, account books, charts, surveys, and field books; and museum material such as pictures, photographs, paintings, portraits, scenes, aboriginal relics, and material objects illustrative of life, conditions, events, and activities of the past and the present.

The society will provide for the preservation of such material and for its accessibility, as far as may be feasible, to all who wish to examine or study it, to co-operate with officials in insuring the preservation and accessibility of the records and archives of the county and of its cities, towns, villages, and institutions, and to undertake the preservation of historic buildings, monuments, and markers.

The society will disseminate historical information and arouse interest in the past by publishing historical material in the newspapers or otherwise; by holding meetings with pageants, addresses, lectures, papers, and discussion; by marking historic buildings, sites, and trails; and by using the media of radio and television to awaken public interest.

The society will co-operate with the state historical society [state historical commission, or state department of archives and history] to collect and preserve materials of state-wide significance so that these materials can be made available to students and scholars.

ARTICLE III
Membership

Membership shall be of five classes:

1. Individual active members—Any person interested in the purposes of the society shall be eligible.

2. Institutional members—Any organization, board, school, or library interested in the history of [specified area] shall be eligible.

3. Contributing and sustaining members—A person, group or firm offering special support to the objectives of the society shall be eligible.

4. Honorary members—Honorary membership may be conferred upon any person whose activities have contributed to the objectives of the society. Honorary members shall be elected by a three-fourths vote of members present at an annual meeting, upon nomination by the board of directors.

5. Life members [individual only].

ARTICLE IV
Annual Meeting

The annual meeting of the society shall be held [during a specified month].

ARTICLE V
Officers and Board of Directors

Section 1. The officers shall be a president, a vice-president, and a secretary, who shall be elected for a term of one year; and a treasurer, and three directors, who shall be elected for a term of three years.

Section 2. The officers and directors shall constitute the board of directors.

ARTICLE VI
Election of Officers and Board of Directors

Section 1. All officers and directors shall be elected by a plurality of votes cast by secret ballot at the annual meeting.

Section 2. Not less than two months prior to the annual meeting, the secretary of the society shall send to each member of the board of directors a blank upon which such member may nominate one person for each office open to election. Nominations shall be returned not less than one month before the annual meeting. A committee on nominations, appointed by the chairman of the board of directors, shall select the candidates from a list of all nominees.

Section 3. Nominations may also be made by any member of the society at any time prior to balloting at the annual meeting. Any nomination made after the deliberation of the committee on nominaions shall be added to the slate of candidates upon affirmative vote of a majority of members present at the annual meeting. A candidate for election shall be an individual active member.

Section 4. A person who has been elected to the board of directors for two consecutive terms, or elected as president or vice-president for three consecutive terms, shall not be nominated to the same office unless one year elapses between the end of his last term and the beginning of the term for which he is nominated.

Section 5. Officers and directors shall be installed at the close of the annual meeting at which they are elected and shall serve until their successors have been duly elected and installed. In the event of resignation or incapacity of any officer except the president, or any director, the vacancy may be filled by a vote of the board of directors for the unexpired term of office.

ARTICLE VII

Amendment

This constitution may be amended at any regular or adjourned meeting by a two-thirds vote of those voting, provided notice was given at the previous meeting. Or it may be amended at a special meeting called for that purpose, with previous notice and a two-thirds vote. All proposed amendments shall be submitted in writing.

APPENDIX III

SAMPLE SET OF BYLAWS

ARTICLE I

Membership and Dues

Section 1. Any person interested in the history of [specified area] who applies for membership in any classification of membership and who tenders the necessary dues shall thereby become a member.

Section 2. Annual dues for individual active members shall be one dollar ($1.00).

Section 3. Annual dues for contributing members shall be five dollars ($5.00).

Section 4. Annual dues for business, institutional, or professional members shall be fifteen dollars ($15.00).

Section 5. Annual dues for sustaining members shall be fifty dollars ($50.00).

Section 6. Dues for life members shall be one hundred dollars ($100.00) in one payment.

Section 7. Annual dues shall be payable in advance, and members in arrears more than six months after payment is due shall be dropped from membership.

ARTICLE II

Schedule and Quorum for Meetings

Section 1. Regular meetings of the society shall be held monthly.

Section 2. Special meetings may be called by the president.

Section 3. The board of directors shall meet every other month. Special meetings of the board of directors may be called by the chairman of the board.

Section 4. One-third of the active members of the society shall constitute a quorum.

ARTICLE III

Duties of the Officers and Directors

Section 1. The president shall have executive supervision over the activities of the society within the scope provided by these bylaws. He shall preside at all meetings. He shall report annually on the activities of the society. He shall appoint the members of committees and delegates not otherwise provided for.

Section 2. The vice-president shall assume the duties of the president in the event of absence, incapacity, or resignation of the president.

Section 3. The secretary shall keep the minutes of meetings of the

36

society and of the board of directors, maintain a list of members, and render an annual report.

Section 4. The treasurer shall be responsible for the safekeeping of society funds and for maintaining adequate financial records. He shall deposit all monies received by him with a reliable banking company in the name of the [official name of the society]. Monies shall be paid out by numbered checks signed by the treasurer and the president. The treasurer will collect dues, and he shall render an annual report based on the calendar year.

Section 5. The board of directors shall have the power to conduct all affairs of the society. It shall select candidates for office, pursuant to the constitution. The board of directors shall decide questions of policy that for any reason cannot be acted upon at a meeting of the society and perform such other functions as designated in the bylaws or otherwise assigned to it.

At any meeting of the board of directors, four members shall constitute a quorum. The board of directors will elect its own chairman. The board of directors, through the chairman, shall render an annual report at each annual meeting.

ARTICLE IV

Committees

Section 1. The society shall have the following standing committees:

1. Library Committee—responsible for collecting, cataloging, the care, arrangement, and repair of books, manuscripts, newspapers, and other historical source material.

2. Museum Committee—responsible for collecting, cataloging, cleaning, repair, and storage of historic objects; for arranging museum exhibits, and the correct historical interpretation of these exhibits; for the care and upkeep of museum quarters.

3. Publications Committee—responsible for finding ways and means for publishing joint or individual research studies; newsletter to members, a quarterly bulletin, or books; for publicity; for staging radio and television programs.

4. Historic Sites Committee—responsible for establishing the historic validity for sites proposed for marking; for marking historic sites; for arranging historical tours.

5. Program Committee—responsible for arranging suitable programs; for setting time, place, and date of meetings.

6. Membership Committee—responsible for membership drives and processing new candidates for membership.

7. Nominations Committee—responsible for making nominations for officers and members of the board of directors.

Section 2. The president shall appoint members and chairmen of the standing committees.

Section 3. Other committees, standing or special, may be appointed by the president as directed by the society or board of directors.

ARTICLE V
Parliamentary Authority

The rules contained in [Robert's *Rules of Order,* Rose Marie Cruzan's *Practical Parliamentary Procedure,* or other authority] shall govern the proceedings of the society except in such cases as are governed by the constitution or the bylaws.

ARTICLE VI
Amendment to the Bylaws

These bylaws may be amended at any regular or adjourned meeting by a two-thirds vote of those voting, provided notice was given at the previous meeting. Or they may be amended at a special meeting called for that purpose, with previous notice and a two-thirds vote. All proposed amendments shall be submitted in writing.

Bulletins of
The American Association
For State and Local History

Directory of Historical Societies and Agencies in the
United States and Canada $3.50

A Guide to the Care & Administration of Manuscripts,
by Lucile M. Kane $1.25

A Handbook on the Care of Paintings,
by Caroline K. Keck $2.00

Archeology and the Historical Society,
by J. C. Harrington $1.00

Interpreting Our Heritage, by Freeman Tilden $1.65

The Management of Small History Museums,
by Carl B. Guthe $1.25

Organizing a Local Historical Society,
by Clement M. Silvestro $1.00

Send orders for Bulletins and a complete list of Technical
Leaflets to:

The American Association for State and Local History
132 Ninth Avenue North
Nashville, Tennessee 37203

AN INVITATION

The American Association for State and Local History is a non-profit educational organization dedicated to advancing knowledge, understanding, and appreciation of localized history in the United States and Canada. It extends to you a cordial invitation to become a member.

The Association, which was founded in 1940, is unique among national historical organizations, both in its emphasis on localized history and in its concerted efforts to serve amateur historians as well as professionally trained scholars. It treats the whole broad spectrum of localized history—from historical museums and historic sites to libraries and manuscript collections, from junior history clubs to the largest historical societies, from elementary school classrooms to university campuses, from village historians to Pulitzer prize-winning authors.

As a member you will receive monthly the Association's magazine, *History News*, which features current activities of state and local historical societies, new ideas and programs, and important new developments in the field. In most issues there is included with the magazine a *Technical Leaflet*, a four to sixteen page how-to-do-it treatment of one of the many specific details of historical society work. You also receive a discount on the purchase of bulletins such as this one, in which leading authorities in the profession discuss major phases of local historical activity. Membership also entitles you to attend the Association's annual meeting and its occasional regional conferences.

For further information on the Association, its membership benefits, and its varied activities, please write:

The Director
American Association for State and Local History
132 Ninth Avenue North
Nashville, Tennessee 37203